To Walk on Eggshells

is to care for a mental illness

Jean Johnston

The Cairn

Published by The Cairn, March 2005.

The Cairn,

Brincliffe,

Dhuhill Drive West,

Helensburgh G84 9AW

www.thecairn.com

A catalogue record of this book is available from the British Library.

ISBN 0 9548092 1 1

Printed by Lightning Source UK, Milton Keynes, England.

Dedication

This is a journey that I could not have made on my own and my sincere thanks go to Alan and our sons Kit and Ollie for simply being themselves. I am deeply indebted to the staff at the Christie Ward, Vale of Leven Hospital and its Community Mental Health Teams along with the GPs and staff of Helensburgh Medical Centre. Finally thanks to Suzy for without her this journey would have been incomplete.

Jean Johnston,
January 2005

Acknowledgements and Thanks

My sincere thanks to the **Scottish Association for Mental Health, Renfrewshire Association for Mental Health, Manic Depressive Fellowship (Scotland), Argyll and Clyde United in Mental Health**, the **Scottish Recovery Network**, the **Scottish Executive's Improving Mental Health and Well-Being Programme** and the **'seeme'** Campaign, for putting up with me and also their encouraging support for The Cairn.

I am indebted to the following for their help and assistance.

Melissa Campbell, Helensburgh – The Cairn logo

Dr Pat Duncan, Rhu - editing

Mark Letham, Clydebank - digital formatting

Claire Letham, Clydebank - artwork and back cover photograph

Paul Morton, fiomultimedia.com, Newcastle - website design

Allan Pollok-Morris Ltd, Herne Hill, London – cover photograph

I first came across Jean when, in a previous job, I started getting phone calls from someone in Helensburgh who appeared to be running an effective campaign to maintain psychiatric services in her area. She seemed to have access to national and local press, high profile supporters, good sources of information and the ear of decision makers and policy bods. When she asked me what she should do I was, not surprisingly, a bit stumped.

Jean's determination, drive and energy are matched only by her incredible modesty – she's often described herself as 'just little me' or 'no expert'. Well the truth is that she is an expert and someone who should be (and is) taken very seriously. She is someone who understands the reality of caring for a person who is experiencing serious mental health difficulties, an able campaigner passionately committed to the importance of high quality treatment services but still recognising the importance of improving awareness of mental health across the whole of society.

Jean's daughter, Suzy, may not have become an accomplished dancer like her mother (there is still time) but Jean's natural writing skills show that some things have been passed down.

With clarity and humour she chronicles her daughter's childhood, teenage years and the eventual descent into severe mental distress. Jean goes on to offer her thoughts, advice and practical suggestions around self-management and recovery from that vital, yet often ignored, perspective – that of the carer.

Simon Bradstreet,
Network Director, Scottish Recovery Network.

It was 14 years ago that Jean Johnston's daughter Suzy developed the first signs of mental illness and the role of mother became that of carer.

Following her recovery from acute mental illness, Suzy Johnston wrote her autobiography 'The Naked Bird Watcher' which is a positive account on living with and learning to manage a mental illness.

'To Walk on Eggshells' is Jean's perspective of that same story.

Jean Johnston lives in Helensburgh, Scotland with her husband Alan. They have two sons and a daughter.

The Cairn of ———————— *Mental Health*

The Cairn, Brincliffe, Dhuhill Drive West, Helensburgh G84 9AW Scotland
www.thecairn.com enquiries – info@thecairn.com

To Walk on Eggshells

We all know the old adage – for better or worse, in sickness and health....etc, etc. Yes – but mental illness? That was never in the remit – there had been absolutely no mention made of it whatsoever.

So whether it was their partner, child or sibling I think most people on being told someone they were related to had a mental illness, would have an initial reaction of – 'you've got WHAT?'

We all have our own ways of dealing with such events. Regardless of what we as individuals might think, at times like these there is no 'right' or 'wrong' way. These are my thoughts on how it was for me as a mum. They are solely my own views which is why I make no mention of the other members of my family. My perceptions may not necessarily be the same as theirs and therefore it would be inappropriate for me to comment on them. Whatever anyone thinks as to how I coped and their opinions on what actions I took– that is up to them. All I can say is that I did the best that I could with the resources and experience at my disposal and with the best of intentions. Most people do not get lessons on being a carer for mental illness – I for one certainly didn't. I'm a pretty straightforward person – what you see is what you get - and this is what mental illness got when it came to call.

Chapter 1

Our early years as a family were happy and untroubled. A comfortable life style – two children born within two years of each other and a 3rd some 6 years later. Those were good times. Happy and well-adjusted children who had a close, loving relationship with each other and all shared an immense pleasure in all form of sport but preferably if it involved a ball.

It was evident very early on that Suzy, our daughter, was not going to follow my love of ballet and dancing – the tears at every dance class were a pretty strong indicator that this was not for her so I abandoned all notion of that within a couple of weeks. Much more to her liking was playing football and swimming with her big brother and the little one who arrived later. Brownies even caused a problem and she left fairly quickly as she would have much preferred to have been a cub but in those days that was not an option.

So there we were with a tom-boy for a daughter and a happy one at that. School did not present any difficulty and an avid reader from an early age she took to learning like the proverbial duck to water. School commented that even from an early age it was evident from her creative writing that she had an extraordinary imagination and unusual capacity to see things differently. She liked to do things as well as she could so she very much enjoyed school and the challenges it would present.

Of a gregarious nature with two brothers as soul mates she had many friends – most of whom seemed to be of a similar sporting bent.

An introduction to squash found her in her ideal environment and with a natural eye and dexterity she showed that she had some talent. With a leading coach taking her on, she was told that to get anywhere as a player she would have to improve her technique. Not one to be easily thwarted, she would diligently throw the ball in the air, hit it and hold her follow through position still in order to check the angles of her body, arms and feet. On being told by the coach if she did that thirty times a session for three weeks she might gain some semblance of a reasonable technique, she chose to do it 50 times everyday for 3 months thereby giving an early indication of her determination and work ethic which until this day has been one of her leading characteristics. She has embraced this philosophy throughout her life – it is not that she has to be the winner or the best – far from it. She just likes to give the things she does her best shot and this has remained her abiding philosophy on life. The squash circuit that was to become a major part of her life gave her a wide range of friends, travel and experiences with her playing at regional and international level and thoroughly enjoying every part of it.

At the age of 13 she become seriously ill and caused us much concern. A mysterious viral condition totally incapacitated her and saw her confined to bed for months on end. These were worrying times. She did not even have the strength to wash her hair herself. Apart from the doctors recommended 20 minutes out of bed daily which sometimes included a gentle walk outside with walking sticks, she rested and slept for days on end. It was to be two terms before she returned to school and gently eased her way back into a normal life. We cut corners not to overtire her and there were lifts in the car everywhere, minimum activities, and lots of rest etc. Through the years she gained something of her former persona. The sporting life had to be modified to accommodate her lack of stamina so she became a goalkeeper as to have denied her any involvement in sport would have totally destroyed her spirit but she treated her health with great respect and recognised her limitations. Like many young people facing serious illness, the experience seemed to have changed her – giving her a maturity and perhaps an awareness of the value of life that the rest of us so readily take for granted.

Chapter 2

Eventually the school years were to be left behind
sadness for they had been happy and secure times. The chapter
on the school days was closing and adulthood was beckoning.
It was time to move on.

For this next chapter of her life Suzy had chosen St Andrews
university and embraced student life with gusto, joining
sporting clubs, making new friends and relishing the challenge
of stimulating study. A slight alteration to her work level was
required when she discovered as she was gaining exemptions
from degree exams she could afford to slacken off a little.

The experience of student life was suiting her and she was
enjoying spreading her wings. She was even seen dancing in a
Madonna cabaret at a university Ball. Having seen the video of
this I am happy to report that she a) had the most clothes on
and b) despite those childhood tears so long ago, she can
actually dance! Good God! (humour me and indulge me for
this moment of a former ballet dancer's maternal pride!) Her
fearless determination on sports fields would see many visits to
casualty but this was not a new occurrence for me and was
something I had come to terms with many years ago as mother
to three intrepid sportsplayers. Having made some great new
friends, new and interesting sports to try out, an active life style
sitting with a comfortable level of studies, university life was

much to her liking and she was a very happy young lady. Everything was as it was meant to be and we were all content.

Chapter 3

I knew something was wrong with our daughter – she was not, to put it bluntly, herself. Was her character changing, was the stress of studying too much, had something happened to her that we didn't know about? Whatever it was something was not right but it was nothing you could put your finger on. But then after a while, she seemed to be back to herself and I would think – yes, she's ok. So when, she told us about seeing a psychiatrist, the first thought was that it would be stress from university except that didn't really fit in with her absolute love of studying and thirst for knowledge. Still, it was the reality perhaps and something we would all have to deal with.

However, things seemed to have settled down and I thought it was something that had passed. She seemed quite perky again. It was only years later that I would discover that my daughter was a great actor. The 'alive' front was just that – a front. Inside she was still engulfed in the torpid grip of depression. The only thing was at this moment in time, none of us knew. Anyway, when it came to the summer break from St Andrews she arrived home. Day after day she would lie on her bed – staring at the ceiling. Student life I thought - is this what happens to all students? I had to cajole her out of bed, jolly her to come to the shops, phone her friends or do anything. What was the hell was going on? How about getting a job? There was not even so much as a flicker.

So here I was – suddenly faced with a daughter who could hardly speak, whose body seemed to have slumped to the floor with a face grey in pallor and accompanied by a total and utter lack of interest in herself, her surroundings or ourselves. And suffering from what she and I now call the classic depression symptom – 'under the duvet syndrome'.

Anyway so we would continue – back to university, periods of good health – further periods of illness and me at a loss as to what to do.

As the periods of depression worsened, we found it hard to understand a) what was wrong and b) and harder still to help.

Visits to psychiatrists, medication – so it would relentlessly proceed and yet there seemed to be no answers, no cures, no help. Difficulties emerged with side effects of the medications – kidney stones, dodgy liver and a zombified young woman who could not drag herself out of bed and yet who wanted to continue being in St Andrews and if possible continue studying.

It was crunch time. Decisions had to be reached, compromises made. The health was so bad that dropping out of university was the only realistic option as the GP felt that Suzy was not 'blooming' in the university lifestyle and she felt that it was this that was the key. Suzy vehemently disagreed with this and a very determined but very ill young lady pleaded to be given the opportunity to stay in the small town. She did this with our support. On occasion I think I understand my daughter and it was my suspicion that if she were removed from this setting it would be the final straw. So, providing I checked on her daily by phone, she could to stay there. You can tell from the tone of her voice as to how she was feeling and it was a gamble that some certainly disapproved of but a choice that we felt was right for her. She had lost her 'being' - if she lost anymore it would finish her.

So there were good times for her and some very, very bad ones which would see me rushing through to be with her to literally keep her safe when the burden of her pain became too great. Without doubt, it was the support and love of her genuinely close circle of friends that made this all possible. Like me, they knew nothing about mental illness when this started. What they could see clearly though was that something was seriously wrong with their friend, and soon they came to understand her and something of the mental pain during the bad times. They gave her space, made no demands, accepting her and her condition just as they found it and like the good friends they were and still are, were there for her when she needed them. Eventually, despite 'dropping out' twice she graduated and to this day, Suzy maintains it was the right thing for her to do.

Another Chapter was over. One that had been a steep learning curve in more ways that we would could have ever imagined. Still despite everything she had achieved the goal she had set herself. Perhaps now things would be easier. Little did we know what lay ahead.

Chapter 4

Leaving your studies behind you is harder than many of us realise. You have left the safe structured timetabled world of school and student life. Suddenly you are 'out there' in that big ocean called the real world. Some students suddenly find they are in rudderless boats - not sure how to steer and in what direction. So it seemed with Suzy. Having developed a love of music through guitar playing she chose to follow a year of developing this skill. Otherwise she had no idea what she wanted to do. Music was obviously her first choice and we respected her viewpoint that if she did not give it a go she would always regret not having tried it. We were happy to encourage her to develop this passion as we had realised early on in her life that Suzy was never going to be conventional. I for one certainly have never envisaged her sitting comfortably in the confines of an office so I have always been prepared for something unusual taking her attention and as the musical dimension of her life was the great love it was one that I was happy for her to try. So she moved from home and worked in a local school to earn some bread and butter while following her musical dream.

But still this 'illness' was haunting her. And there were many dark days, nights and weeks which were pursued by a relentless depression that would not leave her. Doctors were still trying to find answers and medications that would stabilise the condition but to no avail.

Good and happy times intermingled with the bad. But the good times helped us to forget the bad. The year passed and having loved working in a school, she felt that this was where she had a role to play.

Teacher training beckoned and she settled into it well and seemed to have found a vocation that would suit her. Comfortable and happy working with children and sitting with top grades in teaching practice and again with a good circle of friends, perhaps her world would be well now. But no, relentlessly the depression hounded her and we saw her health deteriorate rapidly again. Leaving college made no difference, the depressive grip was becoming tighter and tighter as each month passed.

I will never forget the moment when Suzy told me she was to go into a psychiatric unit. I was in the kitchen and I just burst into tears. It was as if I had been actually physically hit. I didn't think I could take this. I really thought that this is the end and I can't do it anymore. I was shattered. This was utterly out of my domain – I'm her mum and I couldn't help her. Her pain is beyond me and I can't do a thing. I have never ever felt such a total and utter failure in my entire life – and worst of all, the person that I was failing was one of my children.

Chapter 5

Being of a practical nature and having thrown what my family refer to as my normal 20 minute 'wobbly' that I have in moments of crisis, I set to with ironing her pyjamas and to packing her bag. No matter where she was going to a defiant streak in me said that even if she had to go into a psychiatric unit she would go at least go looking clean and tidy! I don't think it takes a psychiatrist or psychologist to work that one out. I was clinging to any vestige of being her mother that I had left. I had to. Right now it was all I could do. So off we set.

To be honest none of us knew what to expect. We arrived at a small freshly painted self contained unit that had just been opened that week. Staff seemed okay but I was in no state to really notice. We seemed to go through some admissions procedures although the only thing I can recall is that I was shaken by the checking of 'sharps' for any self-harming implements. A concept that was totally foreign to me. We were entering a whole new dimension and I was about to do some very fast track learning on the subject of psychiatry and mental illness.

The staff in our unit were amazing – once they got the hang of me and I got the hang of them, I realised that they were there to help. They viewed our family with a degree of suspicion initially but that soon dissipated. I was asked for a background on Suzy due to her comatose state and the staff viewed it with an understandable degree of scepticism. No, our daughter at this moment in time did not look as if she could do anything with a ball never mind captain international teams, read a tabloid never mind study for a degree - or any of the other things I mentioned. As to playing guitar on a stage that would have seemed more than just a tad far fetched. One imagines the day's report commenting on an over ambitious and unrealistic mother!

Anyway this was my introduction to a psychiatric unit and it was to become a long and close relationship. Gradually, a glimmer of the old Suzy was returning and soon she was 'out on pass' and visiting home before being discharged. A Community Psychiatric Nurse would do occasional home visits and hopefully things would improve.

Sadly this was not to be the case and we lurched from that admission to periods of apparent reasonable mental health to another crisis. Gone were the days of tears about a hospital admission – for me it was now a fervent plea that there would be a bed available. And with just cause. This ward was a place of sanctuary and safety – it was what she needed in times of severe depression. One could almost feel the palpable relief in her body language when we opened the Ward door and she felt its security. The relief of not having to fight on alone against the demons that haunted her was overwhelming. It was equalled only by the relief to ourselves. This was the right place – this was where she needed to be to get better.

So the cycle would continue. Hospital, discharge, periods of good health, illness, re-admission – it seemed relentless and it was if we were all treading water and not making any progress. Was this to be our future – a continual revolving door with no way out? And yet the good times were good – really good with a normal full and happy life and I think that is what I found so frustrating. Suzy would be great – doing all that she does, doing it well and seemingly happy – then wham, it would hit it in again for no apparent reason! No triggers, trauma, or anything significant. Only odd bits of stress which seemed to exacerbate the condition and were out of character for someone who until now had enjoyed being put under pressure.

Chapter 6

Another admission – but one which would have very different consequences. She was critically ill on this occasion with medications seemingly doing more harm than good. A severe psychosis that was literally destroying her sanity and her weight was down to seven stone. The outlook indeed looked bleak. There was speculation that recovery of any sort was now not realistic and did we want another opinion? We chose not to because we believed the Consultant and his team seemed to understand Suzy, her case and the problems she faced. We had never met him which surprises people but Suzy and her brothers always saw doctors on their own from about 14 years of age although I was involved in the background when necessary. We all need some control in our lives regardless of any scenario and it is perhaps even more necessary when facing mental illness. Any independence and autonomy with regard to its care is an essential right of the individual. When her condition developed she did not want us directly involved and that has been how we dealt with it. The nurses gave us a degree of information – enough that was reasonable but quite rightly Suzy's relationship with her team is her own business and remains confidential. Her singularly peculiar biochemistry made medication and its dosage very difficult and challenging as she reacts oddly and unpredictably to the prescribed drugs which makes it difficult to find a formula that will suit her health and be tolerable at the same time. Yet it was abundantly clear she needed medication to stabilise the condition. If only that could be sorted out then they could focus on her and the dealing of the condition itself. We knew the professionals were desperate to help her and were themselves distraught at how she was deteriorating. This was a team who were pulling out all the stops and like any psychiatric professionals, keen to make their patient well. Despite her frail state of mind she still felt it was better to be with those who knew her well. She had lost faith in herself, her condition and her treatment and even though her ever-consuming thoughts had taken away her trust of the staff, she still clung to a faint belief that their professional integrity could get her through. To see our daughter tormented by psychotic and delusional thoughts – without trust and consumed by a fear of everyone including her own family was the most harrowing time of all. The deterioration was such that visits were limited to just myself, and the staff even waived the visiting time restrictions to allow me to support her as best I could. What could I do? – nothing really – just be there. I just sat and held her hand for hours on end. Whether she was going to recover or not – she would not be doing it alone. It took three very long and painful months to see some form of normality return and a final discharge.

Chapter 7

It had been a time when everyone involved had learned so very much – patient, professionals, family and friends. We knew that it would take some while for her to recover but none of us envisaged it taking some 18 months. This frail mind needed constant support to build itself again. It wasn't so much that the bricks in the wall had been knocked down and needed to be rebuilt – the actual foundation stones on which the wall was based had gone too. But slowly and surely despite occasional set backs, the rebuilding of what is Suzy started. With the strong support of a very able and caring mental health team, GPs and psychiatrists gradually things improved. There was however this time, a crucial change. Sure at last the right formula of medication had been found, suited her and seemed to work. Sure the depressive episodes still occasional appeared but not like they did in the past. The big difference this time was that it was Suzy herself that was moving forward – she didn't return to the old Suzy who kept it to herself when things were bad. She had learned that to cope with this condition she had to involve others. She was open and upfront about what she was feeling when the depressive episode with its psychotic thoughts came in. Now family and friends have notebooks with instructions about medication to be taken, questions to be asked and action to be taken should it appear. The GPs know the score and (touch wood) it is making such a difference.

Recovery from mental illness for anyone is much harder than most of us realise and not that difficult to understand if you think about it. You would not expect someone to run a marathon immediately on the removal of a plaster cast for a broken leg. The principal is just the same when recuperating from mental illness. Simple things like just talking to people can be inordinately hard, going into a shop on one's own is very challenging, public transport is often the last thing you can manage on your own and certainly for Suzy this was very much the case. But eventually, she was finding her feet mentally.

It was a long and slow process this recovery business but gradually she eased herself into the way of it. Eventually she was well enough to move into a flat with one of her pals and her life went from strength to strength. Yes for her there are the shaky moments when the health wobbles (and whose doesn't?) but she is adept at recognising the signs and takes steps to address them. Whether it is an increase in medication, GP visit or talking to a CPN she seems to have found a way of dealing with her condition. She has a varied and fulfilling life but has learnt to accommodate her condition within it. Her ability to cope with the stress of the challenges that she had loved so much had been seriously undermined by the condition and at long last she recognised that there are some stresses that need to be avoided. So now she will say 'No' to anything if she feels that it is inappropriate or that could be detrimental to her health if a compromise cannot be reached on the arrangement. She evaluates the priorities and decides what she will take on and what she will not. Her strength of character and determination have been huge factors in helping with this positive approach to the self management of her health. So it is toes and fingers crossed, never mind all the other things that are required to stabilise a psychiatric disorder or mental illness.

Chapter 8

I am often asked how I felt when I discovered Suzy had a mental illness. Well I already had realised that something was wrong so it didn't really came as a surprise. To be honest it didn't enter my head 'the mental illness' bit – it was just a case of it was Suzy and she was ill. I have never considered 'mental illness ' and to be honest I don't think as a family that it has ever crossed any of our minds and it is not something which seems to faze us. I have had people say that they could not have coped if one of their children had an episode of mental illness. Really? I dispute that for I think that most people would at least try. For those who say they couldn't I hope they will give the subject some thought and try joining the real world.

For us admittedly it was better once we knew with what we were dealing. At least now there was a reason although we were not sure of the cause. That was to take time.

To be honest, the naming or not-naming of a condition is a debatable subject. For us with a name for the condition of manic depression/bipolar disorder at least we sort of knew what we were dealing with. But others find the labelling painful and non-constructive so I suppose it depends on the individual as to the reaction. I think Suzy is right that at the end of the day it doesn't matter about the name and perhaps we should stop focussing on it so much. Call it an ingrowing toenail if you want to instead of manic depression or schizophrenia but the symptoms will still remain the same. It is the symptoms which matter and it is the dealing with them that helps.

From what I now understand a multitude of illnesses and conditions can have the same symptoms or perhaps some of them. There appears to be a great deal of overlapping with these symptoms and this makes diagnosis very hard but it also means that a variety of medications can be prescribed. Depression for example has a huge range of symptoms which can range from something like 'anxiety' to being high as a kite due to 'an agitated depression'. So remember that there are endless recipes for this dish that is mental illness. If you have depression with psychotic thoughts or delusions you may be prescribed an antipsychotic which is normally given for a condition such a schizophrenia, manic depression etc and that often alarms people. As the mother of a 'consumer' I can assure you on her behalf, that if anything helps the symptoms it is worth trying. As in most illness and conditions of any type, whether physical or mental, there is a varying level of illness from mild to severe. I gave up swotting up and worrying about them all and decided only to deal with what Suzy was having as symptoms. Certainly getting 'hooked' up on and stressed about conditions and medications can be counterproductive and just adds to the stress.

In most situations it is certainly useful to know 'the enemy' so to speak. Learn about it - this mental illness thing: try to understand it although I would only recommend reading and learning about it to a level that you are comfortable with. Seek advice from any resources available either in books, leaflets or from the internet which is a huge source of valuable information - but choose with care. There are a lot of declared non-expert experts out there (I am one myself although I have never claimed to be anything but an enthusiastic amateur) and you will discover that the internet is a bit of a minefield with some charlatans playing on people's vulnerability or with their own views and theories and keen to take advantage of you in furthering their own cause. Also approach with caution anyone who declares to be an expert and now 'knows it all'. You will be given a wide range of views and advice. It is worth taking it with a pinch of salt if only because each case and patient is different and there is no tried and tested formula which will suit everyone. If there were mental illness would surely be a thing of the past. However there is some really good advice to be had with some excellent service-user led sites which are well respected that were set up in the 1990's. The best rule of thumb is anything way out or over the top probably would be worth avoiding.

Certainly, anything that attracts your attention as being a possible help is worth putting by the professionals if you have direct contact with them. It was discovered that Suzy cannot tolerate sugar and eliminating that from her diet helped enormously. Lots of little things like that can make a difference and it is worth looking at altering the life style if it is going to help.

Chapter 9

The subject of medication is a prickly one. It is very hard to prescribe the right medications. Why? Each patient is individual in his or her response to the treatment and also with side effects. Of all areas of medicine, psychiatry faces the most difficulty which if you think about it is no surprise. For a start there are no blood tests, no defining x-rays or monitors to gauge the severity of illness or even diagnose it etc. The side effects of psychiatric medication are legendary and often cause patients to give up taking them. The problems they create are huge and can be even more debilitating than the condition itself on occasion. On the plus side research in psychiatry is advancing so fast that rapid changes with medication are happening the whole time which is encouraging and exciting. Prescribing drugs is very much an area of horses for courses as it is finding out what suits, works and is tolerable in each individual case. It was only through trial and error that an acceptable and tolerable combination of drugs was found for Suzy. Yes they make her tired and so she tries to have a nap in the afternoon or early evening if time allows and if a busy day is on the schedule an early night the day before is a prerequisite. She eats loads of fruit and vegetables to keep herself as healthy as possible to counteract the chemicals she is swallowing and watches her diet to avoid excess weight gain or loss (a common occurrence with psychiatric drugs). She takes Lithium which tends to make people a bit forgetful so she always writes down things, uses a Dictaphone at meetings or in her flat and asks people to put any information she is being given on paper or send it by email too. Of course she curses these side problems and would rather be without them. Who would blame her but she is of the view that she would rather be well despite them and tolerates these inconveniences out of necessity with a remarkable degree of fortitude. As a carer I was given loads of advice by everyone about the pros and cons of 'allowing' our daughter to take so much medication. For a start she may be our daughter but 'allowing' is not within our jurisdiction and hasn't been for a long time – she is an adult and capable of making her own decisions. She recognised even before we did that it was these drugs that were keeping her alive. Some psychiatrists who have treated her say her condition is of a very clinical nature (ie it is due to chemical imbalances) and it will always be dependent on medication. Whatever viral thing she had in her teens seems to have caused a problem while she herself has had to make some alterations to her lifestyle to avoid becoming ill. No matter what is ultimately responsible her biochemistry does not appear to be as it should be. As she so eloquently put it to one Consultant, it is 'totally f....d up' and startled he spluttered in agreement that he couldn't put it better himself! Yes it took time to get the meds right but that was no-one's fault - just the nature of psychiatry and her own peculiar biochemistry. So having advice like 'if she was my daughter I'd get her off all these medicines' was not really helpful. Nor was 'take her off to get her some sunshine and she'll soon perk up'. So as you struggle to deal with your problems you have the additional burden of justifying it to those who know you. Something you could do without really although people are meaning well and trying to be helpful.

So what is this person who is a psychiatrist working with? Most likely it will be only the patient's behaviour and what the patient is saying about what is going on in the head. Now I don't know about you but if I had been in the same sort of distress as Suzy was, I don't think I would want to be telling anyone about what was going on in my head either. Being a psychiatrist could be rather an uphill struggle I suspect. Imagine facing patients who don't trust you because they are so ill and may be psychotic or delusional, then carers who don't trust you because you are prescribing all sorts of zombifying medicines to their loved one or you are the ogre who sanctions Sectioning. Yet, these Consultants see patients getting better and often get little thanks. Would you want to do what seems at times to be such a thankless task? Still there have been times within the confines of an acute psychiatric ward when I have seen these men and women almost performing miracles as they go about their healing.

My personal experiences are that psychiatric nurses are a breed apart. Carers know that dealing with one person with a mental illness is daunting and challenging enough – multiply that with a Ward or a case list of 24 and you will get the picture. Then they have us the stressed, over anxious, worried, angry or intimidating carers to deal with. Not exactly the most enviable of workloads if you stop to think about it.

By and large the majority of those who go into the mental health profession tend to be good and decent people. So I can suggest something - they are NOT the enemy. The patient and you might not see that and think that the professionals are trying to be obstructive and put hurdles in your way, making life harder but far from it. They are on your side and that of the patient, though for many when they are in a time of crisis, they cannot see it. They are there to help this injured and troubled mind. They do not want people to be ill, they do not want to delay someone's recovery. Their priority is the patient and carers sometimes need to be reminded of that. Their job is hugely complex, hard and demanding. And they – the staff - are like the rest of us – they are only human and have consciences too - being moved and deeply affected by what happens in their working lives. Trust me, I have had many years of dealing with mental health professionals and I know that it takes someone very special to do this job for starters. So sure the patient or carer may not like them but very few people who go into the psychiatric profession are nasty by nature. In some cases they are working in appalling conditions – under-staffed, overworked with long hours and often in far from ideal conditions. We may be fighting against such things on the patients' behalf but it is worth bearing in mind that they are the staff's workplaces too and some of them are pretty grim. They are troubled by what happens to their charges too – just as carers are. However they do not do the 24/7 care that is the lot of the carers. And as carers with experiences of mental illness know mental illness tends not to take time off for weekends or bank holidays. It most definitely does not do annual leave. An appointment to see a professional in two weeks, never mind a year if it is a psychologist, is of absolutely no use if you are in the midst of an acute crisis. It is 'now' that matters at such times. However, the 'system' is starting to address these weaknesses which can only be of help for the carer and patient. At last there is a recognition within the profession that the demands on carers are at times intolerable and detrimental to both patient and carer. It will take time, money and effort to put into place mechanisms that will benefit everyone but at least there are now signs of dialogue and consultation. If things are to change, patients and carers should be listened to as they have a valuable and constructive contribution to make if conditions and the mental health services are to be improved.

Unlike other areas of illness mental illness is different in that the unpredictability of times of crisis means such luxuries as respite are difficult to plan and are even more difficult to get.

Certainly I have valued the professionals as the key components in our care strategy. Yes, there was a time when I was perhaps the key player in Suzy's care but not any longer. The professionals have been my allies and I have had the greatest respect and regard for their role. They have taught me much and I don't think they will ever realise to what extent I owe them.

However I am only too well aware that our experiences have been the exception rather than the rule. All is not well in the world that is the care of the mentally ill. There are plenty of horror stories about inappropriate care and treatment and it is vital that these inadequacies are addressed urgently for in some cases the care has been appalling. If you are faced with such problems or things that are not in the patient's best interest you can take action. Do it through the proper procedures and channels to voice your concern. Perhaps a member of staff and the patient have taken an instant dislike to each other (it does happen) and if there is such a problem the patient is entitled to ask to be seen by someone else - though being civilised about your request obviously helps. There are protocols and procedures set in place to address any unprofessional behaviour or unacceptable conduct. Use these if you have an issue that you wish to raise. Right now falling out with people is just going to be an additional stress you could do well without. Naturally it is instinct to apportion blame for what is happening but try to keep it in perspective. Advocacy is usually available and can advise you on what steps to take if such a situation arises. Human nature is such that there will always be areas of personal conflict and psychiatry is no different. This may come as a surprise to you but carers and patients aren't perfect either. So perhaps the difficulties could, on occasion, be of our own making and perhaps at times if we could see the other sides point of view it would help. It could be that the professionals had a legitimate reason for what has happened. However I am still under no illusions, the dangers of bad or inappropriate mental health nursing or psychiatry are immense and do untold long term harm and can destroy what is the final vestige of a life. It has to be brought out into the open when it is evident. There are many aspects that need to be addressed and these changes must continue.

My bone of contention is that if someone like Suzy can receive exemplary psychiatric care within the NHS it proves it can be done. Therefore it should be and must be the right of everyone to have the same.

Chapter 10

Most of us have heard of self-harm although I had only ever had first hand experience of it when Suzy was being admitted to hospital and the staff checked for 'sharps' but then I didn't appreciate the implications. I was at this time of my life in essence something of a 'psychiatric virgin'. My how times have changed!

In all honesty, discovering that Suzy was self-harming was not that much of a surprise. This was probably because as she was in such evident mental torment and anguish that I don't think there was anything left to surprise me. I listened to her, her reasoning and totally understood what drove her to do it. She was cutting herself secretly with razor blades. Not in a major way as she didn't want to be found out and also she was a bit of a coward too she told me. I didn't like it and I certainly didn't feel very good inside myself about it either as I found the idea that my daughter was taking a razor to harm herself quite hard to get my head round. However it was obvious that her pain and torment was such that she was reduced to doing this so I did respect her stand on it.

Self-harming is a complex issue and by all accounts it seems to be a symptom of underlying issues as well as a coping strategy. It affects either sex and all age groups – including middle-aged and the elderly.

47

Self-harm comes in all shapes and sizes of methods. It can include cutting, burning, swallowing harmful substances, self battering, and hair pulling along with not eating or self induced vomiting (anorexia and bulimia). If you want to get really analytical and debate the issues you could also add drinking to excess, drugs and smoking. Whatever the triggers are it is far more common that any of us realise. We are also facing a deeply troubled young generation and I am no authority on the whys and wherefores that afflicts it. All I know is the signs are there and we would be wise to watch out for them. Certainly school teachers are reporting a huge increase of it happening amongst their pupils and it is so prevalent that there is now a national enquiry carrying out a comprehensive investigation throughout the UK. Be warned, self-harming should not be dismissed out of hand and treated flippantly – it is a sign that all is not well and requires respect and careful handling.

There is absolutely no point in being sanctimonious and saying 'my son/daughter would never self-harm'! They do and our one did and yet those who knew her would never have considered Suzy as a potential candidate but that was what she was.

The good news is that she stopped and it is important to ask why. It wasn't because we asked her not to do it. Suzy cut herself because of how she was feeling and it was only because she developed coping strategies that allowed her to find a way of dealing with her pain and its difficulties that the cutting stopped. Hopefully those similarly affected will find an equally healthy alternative way to deal with the painful issues that are causing them to hurt themselves.

Chapter 11

The Family – what about the poor old family involved in this?
Family life still goes on – brothers and sisters their lives
continue and they will have their own issues of growing up to
deal with and the stresses that it encompasses. Add to that the
burden of living in an environment pained by mental illness. It
is a lot to ask of anyone. The impact on family members when
dealing with a mental illness/psychiatric disorder is immense
and don't ever underrate it. It is unlikely at the start that any of
you know what is going on and life does tend to get pretty
tense. Even once you know what you are dealing with there is a
deepset mixture of fear, anger, confusion, uncertainty and
possible resentment. Our youngest was only 12 when his
adored big sister became ill. A lot to ask of anyone never mind
someone one that young. Not once throughout these years did
he falter or waiver and it is not for nothing that is he known
within this family as 'The Rock'.

This is when it is important to remember we are individual and
respond to things in our own unique way. For brothers and
sisters it can be bewildering, frightening and scary when such
illness strikes a family member. If aggressive behaviour is a
symptom it will be very frightening. When a severe depression
is present one lives in fear of saying the wrong thing and
making things worse. It is quite simply as if you are *walking on*

eggshells. Anything you say or do can be taken the wrong way and do untold harm or damage so you pussyfoot around tentatively making comments in the hope that you do not make things worse. So we find a whole family living under enormous stress, strain and on edge. Thoughts race round the family members' minds – will I develop this too, what if he/she does not get better, what of the future, whose fault is it and what caused it, was it me and what I did as a parent? – and so it goes on. An endless quest of self-punishing questions. The strain of worry on the carer makes the carer even more edgy so things are compounded with patience and tolerance being tested to the core. In many households tempers erupt. As far as I am aware I didn't blow a gasket as such but I do know I would perhaps get cross or angry about something that was relatively minor or trivial. I was lucky in that the family realised this and we all recognised and respected that we were all just as worried as each other. In some houses the tension must be unbelievable and unbearable. The resentment could be huge and guilt trips are the norm. And God it is so tiring. You are literally living your life on a knife edge. Mental illness can go on and on for it tends not to respond quickly to treatment so it is unlike any other kind of illness. For starters you can't see it. It is the utter helplessness of it all that knocks you sideways. No, making a hot drink won't help, a painkiller won't take away the pain and a hot-water bottle won't relieve the ache. I'll never forget that feeling of uselessness. Yes, you cry at 3.00 in the morning, you beg God to give you this pain rather than let her suffering continue. You make promises, you make deals and bargains. You will do anything. At times you rant and rage while inwardly you quietly grieve for that which is lost. You feel so many different things and that in itself is exhausting. It is dealing with mental illness and I would think that the reaction is normal.

We all rise to these challenges in different ways and I can't recommend a sure way of what is the right thing to do. You have to work out yourself. Do what suits you. Me – well I am a talker and a thinker and I do both rather a lot. So talking about it helps me but also I needed time on my own and some space. I enjoy my own company quite a lot, finding it helps to recharge my batteries mentally and emotionally. Every day if I could, I would always go for walk - on my own so I could just think things through - and afterwards meet for coffee with a very dear and undemanding friend who listened – one who never passed judgement or comment but let me twitter on as I do. We would also blether about this and that – for me this was not only a godsend but probably a necessary therapy. If you can manage it, try and do what it is that will help you. Something that will give you some pleasure. I won't go so far as calling it quality time but do find some. Whatever it is and regardless how you define it – make it YOURS. Some people prefer to go out and socialise whereas for me it would just do my head in trying to be the life and soul of a party while living under such a strain. Whether parents or partners we cannot be all things to all people all of the time and that is something we easily forget. A recharged carer is of more use and value than one that is a worn out and frazzled emotional wreck. This is a time when tempers are frayed, you are overtired and it does not take much to rock the boat. Blowing a fuse at the slightest incident is really not going to be helpful right now.

The problem for the carer and the crux of the matter of course is that mental illness does not take breaks. It can go on 24 hours a day for day after day after day and that is when it is so hard to cope. Only those who have lived the experience of living with someone in mental distress know that you just DARE NOT take that much needed break and so people stagger on as best they can waiting for the episode to pass. Why dare you not take a break at this time you may well ask? Because you can't. These are dangerous times and the consequences of them could be fatal. If your daughter was having suicidal thoughts over which she had no control would you leave her on her own? I think not. It is as simple as that.

Chapter 12

So what do I think of mental illness itself?

Shit! And I make no apology for that. The truth is that I think mental illness can be total shit. At times it is a hellish and a diabolical condition. It is insidious, perverse, sneaky and it destroys all semblance of self worth. It causes untold misery and pain. It destroys the lives of those it holds within its grasp and those affected by these lives. It not only break minds, it breaks hearts too. It shatters dreams. For a carer it is so hard to get to grips with a mental illness and understand what it does. For a start you cannot see it and you cannot understand it. You don't know what to do or how to act and it further contaminates the lives of those that live with it in their midst.

It is deadly and it is a killer.

So yes at times I do hate it. As illnesses go never underestimate this one - it is a condition that commands and demands the utmost respect.

By its very nature it is isolating, self-absorbing and selfish. It is not that patients do not care about anything or anyone – it is just that their illness makes them incapable of such thoughtful consideration. These mentally distorted thoughts, particularly psychotic ones, totally dominate and seem so real that no amount of reasoning will diminish them. The lack of concern for others is not a selfish action; it is just the total belief in the reality of the overwhelming thoughts that are absorbing this unwell mind. They do not reflect what the well person would normally think or feel. It is at times like this that you are quite literally having '*to walk on eggshells*'. The wrong word or careless remark so easily can do damage. Say a comment an hour later and it will be fine, say it now and the patient will interpret it in some bad way. Trying to be this sensitive as to how the patient will react to what you are saying or doing is an enormous strain under which to live and is hard to appreciate through lack of insight. Perhaps it is only when you have been 'there' either personally or as a close companion on that terrible journey that you appreciate the significance and dangerous implications of this symptom. There are times when even the professionals often 'don't get it'. A simple example could be that if I said to someone who was seriously psychotic that I have a beautiful long black evening dress, all that person will recall is black. So all they would recall of our conversation is that there was something black about me and it was sinister and evil. I have over simplified this example but some say that that this is exactly how they think when they are ill. So basically it seems that a patient tends to focus on anything negative and ignore what is positive. This is enormously hard to understand, never mind handle and I am still learning just how important things like this are. There will be times when everything you say or do really has to be analysed for its potential consequences.

At least we did not have to deal with the anguish of mania – with that the load is intolerable with people so deranged by their thoughts that they are totally out of control and it is impossible to reason with them. That is a truly difficult symptom to handle and it can have the most awful of repercussions.

In reality one of the greatest attributes a carer is going need is patience. On average mental illness does not normally do quick fixes. It is not just the patient who will require patience and it is a characteristic that I am not strong on either. So I had to learn the hard way and I suppose I just sort of became resigned to the inevitability of it all. Certainly whatever I thought or felt was not going to make a difference and it was clear that this was going to take time. So an impatient carer does not help and in fact it will probably only do more harm.

One of the plus points throughout these experiences is that I have met the most amazing people and made some wonderful friends. The common bond of mental torment gives a unique relationship to those it affects and we have encountered some smashing people on this extraordinary journey that we met on the way. I also have the highest regard and respect for those who work within the profession. Not only for their dedication to their work but the difficulties and uncertainties they face as the mental health services make the necessary adjustments as they deal with the 21st century.

I have learnt so much over these long years and was blessed with good teachers in the shape of Suzy, the Christie Ward staff and the CPNs (Community Psychiatric Nurses) but I acknowledge that perhaps I have been especially fortunate. Suzy's unusually clear insight into her condition is an enormous benefit in managing it – many are not so blessed and I do feel for them and those that care about them. In her autobiography 'The Naked Bird Watcher' she articulates the pain of mental illness frighteningly well. Imagine then living in such anguish. Imagine then having to watch your own loved one live within that torment. That is the lot of the carer.

On the plus side I don't just love our daughter, I happen to like her too and we have always got on well. Through her I have been privy to a revealing glimpse of this agony. From her I have learned so much about this pain as well as from the others I met over the years and who have become good and valued friends. But I, like all those involved in mental health, will continue to learn for there is no such thing as total 'expertise' – there is 'academic knowledge' and 'personal experience' and for both factions it will always be an ongoing learning process. Hopefully together they can strive for the betterment of the care of the mentally ill.

When we embarked on this journey I think perhaps the worst aspect of it was the not knowing about what was going on. Like most people let me know what I'm dealing with and I'll get my head round it, face up to it and deal with it as best as I can. But this was different from the start in that it took such a very long time to come to a conclusion as to what was the actual problem. Then, of course, there are the restrictions of patient confidentiality. If the patient does not want you to know anything about their case then that is how it will be. The difficulty is that when the person is discharged, he/she is likely to be returning to living with the carer and perhaps the carer is not included in the patient confidentiality. So we may have the position of still an acutely ill person with a carer ignorant of what is happening and who is unable to recognise what the indicators of a deterioration in health are, or what he/she should be doing to help – whether to back off or encourage activity, give the patient space etc or what. This is a very tricky time and it should be remembered that in most other areas of medicine often you will be given guidelines and advice for the care of a recuperative patient following a hospital discharge. In this one you don't.

Suzy and I dealt with this by me sounding her out as to what she thought she could or could not do. For example a trip to town could not be managed as she did not want to face the ordeal of public transport. First I took her by car, next I would go on the train with her. Having a haircut was arranged for when the hairdresser was quiet and not busy. By compromising as much as possible we could gradually make some headway, and increase the challenges as we progressed.

Of course there were setbacks on the way. Many to be honest and they are inevitable. But pass they will – for bad times occur but they can be managed. In our case we battened down the hatches, lived quietly and waited for her to ride it through. It is very draining being the 'optimistic' voice all the time and making reassuring sounds that this will pass. How well I recall the phrase 'and this too will pass' although to be honest there were times when my 'optimism battery' ran a bit flat. When that happened I would look back and remind us of the worst of times and then we would see that things were indeed getting better. So yes, someone could not cope with being in the city for the day. But if you looked back perhaps there was a time they could not have even got into the city in the first place so the fact that they had got there themselves on that day in itself was an achievement. So imperceptibly progress is being made. We also found that some humour helped too and for us it is a good way of sometimes getting a message across.

'Get off my case, Mum' meant don't fuss mother.

While "How're you doing men'lly?" (quite frequently there is not a 'T' in mental where I am concerned!) or "how's your head?' gave her the opening to say how she really was feeling. Bit by bit we made headway.

It is just that the goals being set needed to be realistic and achievable. And if it they are not, perhaps a compromise of expectation has to be made with a life altered to accommodate what has happened with adjustments and achievable aims. Normally we all have varying degrees of what we do or don't do. The same applies to mental illness. What one person considers a recovery will be different to another's. Remember it is as people that we are different, not just illnesses or conditions.

The whole of life is about compromises and we all have to make them with parents having to accept their children for what they are and not what they want them to be. The same applies to us all in most of our relationships. As a parent you prepare your offspring to live in an ever changing and unpredictable world. Often it has to be for a world you perhaps did not expect. Like most parents, we have tried to prepare our children to cope with life and what it will throw at them. Unfortunately as we know the job description does not come with training – learning on the job is a prerequisite and mistakes are bound to happen. The same applies to those who may have any off spring who have an additional burden and although it took sometime to get grips with our daughter's burden we as a family got there.

I appreciate that we have been extraordinarily fortunate in what we have had to deal with. We have been lucky that it was a condition that eventually responded to medication, that our daughter is keen to avoid periods of illness and has developed coping skills to deal with them. We also know we were hugely lucky in Suzy herself. Many have commented on the fact that as a person she has an inner strength, integrity and vision which set her apart – a very peculiar but intriguing mix of modern young rock chick, a fine mind, great humour and wit but with a strong old fashioned morality and goodness that sit oddly but so very comfortably together. Perhaps though it was to be these very qualities and characteristics that would make it so hard for her to deal with the condition in the first place. Who knows? But nowadays whatever the mixture is, I am glad she has it. But I certainly have never considered her to be 'perfect' – in fact in some areas she is honestly anything but and like the rest of us she is only human.

When patients get better often people say that 'someone is back to their old self' and in some cases that is ok. For others it is not, for if they go back to what they were it may ultimately lead to the same events, situations and reactions again and subsequently they may become ill again. What Suzy did was that she had to move forward. She now lives a life to accommodate her condition and respects that she has to do this. Her motto is 'that to move forward is to have the ability to look back and not make the same mistakes again'. Now she realises that she needs plenty of sleep, a healthy diet and that for her, in all probability for the rest of her days, medication will be a life-saver. Should she forget to take her meds her health is affected within hours so she knows only too well how important it is. She is comfortable with that and would rather deal with these constraints than the alternative.

As to mental illness – it must be emphasised that the majority of people will only have a one off episode – an isolated event and then they will recover. Others perhaps will have periods of illness at intermittent intervals and also with varying degrees of severity. The majority will recover and there is reason for optimism. I am fully aware that our level of illness was of a severe nature but still there was a recovery. Certainly Suzy found that St Andrews University was extremely supportive and understanding but perhaps this was because she told the staff what was going on from the very start. Certainly for this student the understanding and respect from one particular philosophy lecturer was crucial and much appreciated. Maybe she was lucky but perhaps it would be easier employment-wise etc if all those involved were aware of the situation from the beginning so there is understanding with appropriate allowances being made to accommodate a proper recovery – not just from an illness or condition but an actual life-style.

Mental illness is often gauged by statistics. And it is damnable. Well, I don't want or consider my daughter to be a statistic – she is not a digit or just a number on a line. Each and every number that is so represented is someone's partner, mother, father, brother, sister or friend. This is what motivates me to try and help. I know full well that Suzy would never kill herself – but the condition could so if I can give a hand (albeit it is a little and unqualified hand) to anyone I know who is in mental distress, I will do so to the best of my ability – day or night.

Like most mothers, I'll try anything to keep my family safe and well so you may identify with the following. There was a time I had blonde highlights in my hair. You'll understand that I had cancelled my hair appointment to get them done when Suzy went into hospital and said I would make an appointment when she was better. As her condition deteriorated, I found myself chatting to God on the drive from the hospital one night (as you do), saying that if he would just let her get better and never let her be that ill again, I would never do anything to my hair colour again. I am a woman of my word, stuck to the promise – Suzy is well and her condition is stable and I am grey. On hearing this a Consultant remarked 'so it's nothing to do with medication or treatment then?'

Suzy replied, 'Of course it is, but being my mum she's just not taking any chances!'

Chapter 13

Sometimes it is not just the patient who has to alter the life style. The carer or the family has to adapt too and change the relationship's dynamics or role. Perhaps it is not only the person who has been ill that has to move forward. It is hard to let go but if things are to progress it is necessary. Ultimately regardless of any mental illness or condition the view of the professionals is that the patient is responsible for him/herself and that is how it should be. Anyway it is something we all should be doing with our lives as we progress regardless of circumstances. We should all be moving on. For one I was more than happy to do so. There comes a time when it is right to let go.

Whatever the outcomes of your own experiences it is important to remember that they are yours and we are all so different in anything we do in our lives - be it at school, work or life itself. In mental illness it is easy to forget that these differences apply here too so there is no use in saying so and so is doing this or got over that so why can't you? Mental illness is so individual to each person that no two cases are alike and perhaps that is one of the most frustrating things from the carer's point of view. So what has worked for us, will not necessarily to suit your situation.

So why did I write this. Only because 14 years ago I just felt so alone and isolated, unaware that there were others who were facing the same long haul. Like most of us I did not envisage what lay ahead. I knew damn all about mental illness and even less about how to help. For that matter neither did my friends and initially really there was nowhere to turn. To be honest it is not exactly something you are going to be rushing around telling everyone about. So perhaps if reading this gives some insight and hints on what to do or say as a friend, it might be a help. Certainly with hindsight perhaps I should have spoken to my GPs but I chose not as I was only just keeping it together and did not want to risk cracking up myself. This was a moment in my life that I had to be strong. There was no choice. Certainly I would suggest that this is a burden you cannot carry on your own and I would strongly recommend you confide in someone – be it a GP, a member of the staff, a minister or priest or what ever. But often it will be another carer who is in the same situation. The common bond you share may be of help. There will be someone somewhere that you can talk over how you are feeling. I found the ward cleaner in the Christie Ward extremely easy to talk to and as a member of her family had schizophrenia she more than empathised with how I was feeling. She was a great help and to me she made a big difference. Whoever it is, it is the empathy factor that is the key.

Carers are only human too and we tend to forget that. It could be worth finding a support group or organisation that you could join and you may find it a help. Psychiatric nurses are a good source for places to get all sorts of help and they could give some guidance. This account may or may not have helped you but I hope it gives some insight to another carer's perspective. As you can imagine writing this has not been particularly easy and it has been somewhat painful but I won't make such cringe making worthy comments that if writing this helps someone else then our suffering will have been worthwhile. Utter rubbish! I'm a mother for goodness sake, and just as any other mother would have done, I would have fought tooth and nail for my daughter not to have gone through this horrendous suffering. But help is out there – you just need to find it. There are all sorts of groups and regardless of their actual activities you may find some soul mates and a little respite from your worries. The information should be available at medical centres, hospitals, churches, community centres and libraries and in local newspapers. I certainly think fellow carers can often give solace to each other – especially when it is about mental illness.

Chapter 14

So where am I now? Well for my sins I am involved in mental health. Why on earth you may ask? For a variety of reasons.

Primarily it is because I care passionately and deeply about mental health/illness. Having nearly lost my daughter through it and been at the receiving end of good psychiatric care, I want that level of care to be the right of everyone and hopefully some people will learn from our experiences.

I also want it to be obligatory for the powers that be to listen to the views of service-users/carers and involve them in the actual design process of any future service changes. Right now the care of mental health is changing dramatically and while it is still in tricky waters and at the time of writing it could be said that ours are rather more than just turbulent, I hope, given the opportunity and the right circumstances, that this time of change could be an exciting and constructive one. I am encouraged that there is at least recognition that the input of patients and carers could be of crucial value as the services are restructured. Certainly Care in the Community is the way forward and with a compromise of some inpatient care along with an acceptable level of supported service it requires, this could be the answer. Only time will tell. The promises that are being made will only provide the answers if they are kept.

We all have physical health, which we are more than happy to talk about and sympathise when it goes wrong.

What really hacks me off is that we all also have mental health, which we chose to ignore. One in four of us will require medical help when IT goes wrong – only we can't or don't like to talk about it! What is our problem? Why are we so ashamed of it? Why is it perceived as a weakness? Why do we discriminate without insight or knowledge? To me it all seems to stem from ignorance. Fear of the unknown is the greatest fear of all and raising awareness could well be the key to solving this dilemma.

We may not have the answers yet for the provision of mental health care but at least Scotland has had the gumption and the initiative to courageously grasp the thorny thistle that is mental illness. In order to address the issues of mental health, The Scottish Executive through its Mental Health Division has invested in developing in the National Programme for Improving Mental Health and Well-Being in Scotland. The various Divisions of this Programme include 'Choose Life Initiative', 'Breathing Space', 'seeme Campaign', 'Well' Magazine, and 'Scottish Recovery Network' along with 'Mental Health First Aid' as well as putting in place funding for related projects. The challenges of raising mental health awareness are huge for sadly as a topic it does not hold a lot of consumer appeal. It will take a great deal of enterprise and more than just a little creative thinking to capture the minds, never mind the souls, of such an entrenched prejudiced nation. However, there are encouraging chinks of light that glimmer through the dark and inroads are being made so there is reason for optimism despite some on-going issues, which will require to be addressed.

I confess that as I fight in my patch to maintain a reasonable and safe mental health service and hear of patients being unable to obtain beds or access emergency help, it can irk and vex me at times that we have to invest in promoting mental health awareness. The reality is that I am at the coal face and keep an eye on a group of people who need a properly functioning mental health service. At present it more than just aggrieves me when the lack of a bed or crisis service results in untold suffering or the stark statistic that is yet another death. Who would not feel the same? But needs must if we are to make headway so if raising awareness finds people addressing their mental health issues sooner rather than later – then that can only be to the good.

Yet when I make mention of mental illness when I am out and about you can bet your bottom dollar that someone within the group will comment that they have a friend or relative with a related condition. What does alarm and sadden me is that everyone seemed so relieved that they could finally talk about it. So as to mental health awareness, it would seem that much still needs to be done.

I do believe though that it will be by raising awareness that the differences will be made. Suzy and I, in our own small way, have committed ourselves to this strategy. Suzy formed The Cairn in June 2004 and now writes, advises, promotes and publishes on mental health awareness issues. I help out as best I can. The interest and support from the leading mental health organisations has been great and is much appreciated. Since starting The Cairn some six months ago, Suzy has been delighted and flattered at the invitations to work on so many leading mental health programmes, magazines and with the media so these are encouraging and exciting times. A recent visit to Denmark to meet with psychiatrists was deemed a great success with a further invitation to return in the Spring. The open invitations from the States and further afield will take careful planning for they would need to be co-ordinated to involve a stay of decent length to accommodate the health and the difficulties that long haul travel presents.

As those who already know us realise, we are pretty upfront and I suppose I am rather 'in your face' about mental illness and see it in rather 'a matter of fact' way. Although as people we are vastly different, Suzy and I seem to be quite effective as a team when it comes to the subject of mental health awareness issues. What with me being a bit of a loose cannon she counters me well by being a very level headed and perceptive cruise missile. She is most definitely the boss who reins me in when required but I am very much the campaigner and profile raiser while she is the communicator and educator.

So hopefully we can make a small difference and help to bring mental health up to date and gosh there are still times when it needs it. Why not? We have friends who live with diabetes, kidney dialysis, etc – for them there is no talk of 'enduring, chronic, survivors or problems'. The symptoms of mental illness are horrendous and I would never make light of that burden but the people themselves are not the burden - it is their condition that is and as a society we tend to be confused about that. The language attributed to mental illness perhaps in itself is a disservice in that it seems to enhance the discrimination and stigma. We still have an archaic mindset in this the 21st Century when we talk on the subject. Anyway it is our hope that we can make our own positive and constructive contribution in addressing these issues and that the role of 'The Naked Bird Watcher' and her mum will be of some value.

Epilogue

By its nature this was a long and arduous journey so I have deliberately kept its account short in the hope that the reader has not been bogged down by some rather heavy and painful reading. I hope though that by condensing such an epic voyage I have in no way diminished the magnitude of it.

These days Suzy is an able, independent and determined young woman with a calm but firm resolve to be her own person and follow her chosen path. She leads a full and varied life doing the things that she wants to do. I suppose with hindsight our journey has been one of 'recovery' but it is just we did not know then that it had such a name. Although nameless it was still to be a journey that offered hope.

These days I am secure in the knowledge that should her health ever again falter, Suzy now has a network of mental health professionals, GPs and good friends who are there for her should she ever need their support.

I am no longer a carer - I am back to being 'mum'. It is as it should be.

The End

The Naked Bird
Watcher
Suzy Johnston

In an engaging, informative and often amusing autobiography, what continually shines through is the author's consistently positive outlook and her refusal to be ashamed of losing what she describes as 'the battle of percentages' in developing manic depression. In this candid and honest description of one person's experience of living a full and varied life whilst coping with a serious mental health problem, the author gives a vividly graphic but lucid insight into the torment that is mental distress. The author highlights the importance of good and appropriate psychiatric treatment, the role of support and the value of good self management as being the vital aids to recovery and mental health stability. This autobiography will not only be of interest and help to those within and connected to the mental health professions and service users but also the lay person and public at large. One of the author's aims of writing this book was to challenge the mindless and enduring stigma associated with mental health problems, pointing out that people who battle daily with mental illness are worthy of applause rather than being discussed in embarrassed tones – as she puts it: 'bollocks to that'.

'The Naked Bird Watcher' by Suzy Johnston, published by The Cairn ISBN 09548092 0 3 price: £10.00 – Available from The Cairn – www.thecairn.com, bookshops and Internet book sites.

Printed in the United Kingdom
by Lightning Source UK Ltd.
109559UKS00002B/139-147